KT-556-022

LD 4113003 0

CHANGES IN
CLIMATE

QED Publishing

Copyright © QED Publishing 2009

First published in the UK in 2009 by
QED Publishing
A Quarto Group Company
226 City Road
London EC1V 2TT
www.qed-publishing.co.uk

All rights reserved. No part of this publication may be reproduced, stored in a retrieval system, or transmitted in any form or by any means, electronic, mechanical, photocopying, recording, or otherwise, without the prior permission of the publisher, nor be otherwise circulated in any form of binding or cover other than that in which it is published and without a similar condition being imposed on the subsequent purchaser.

ISBN 978 1 84835 187 5

Author Steve Parker
Consultant Terry Jennings
Project Editor Anya Wilson
Design and Picture Research
    Dynamo Design

Publisher Steve Evans
Creative Director Zeta Davies
Managing Editor Amanda Askew

Printed and bound in China

Picture credits

(t=top, b=bottom, l=left, r=right, c=centre, fc=front cover)

Corbis 4b Vincent Laforet/Pool, 22b Burma News Agency, 24l Ashley Cooper, 24–25 Marco Simoni, 27tr Tim Pannell, 27b Kevin Dodge, 29t Terry W Eggers

Getty 15tr Clin Keates, 18b Jason Hawkes, 20–21 Dan Knitwood/staff, 21tr Tariq Dajani, 22–23 US Air Force/ Science Faction, 29bl AFP/Stringer

NASA 23 tr

Shutterstock 4b Phase4Photography, 4t Pepita, 4–5 Hywit Dimyadi, 4l Martine Oger, 4br Peter Blottman, 5t Andreas Meyer, 5lb Nikolay Okhitin, 5r kkaplin, 5br Tischenko Irina, 6l Dr Morley Read, 7r Hugo de Wolf, 7b Galyna Andrushko, 7br Hirlesteanu Constantin-Ciprian, 8–9 Alex Staroseltsev, 9r patrimonio, 10–11 Serg Zastavkin, 10br Andrey Pavlov, 11br Peter Zaharov, 12–13 Mark William Richardson, 12r yanik Chauvin, 13t nmedia, 14br Tom Grundy, 15br Yvan, 14–15 Stephen Aaron Rees, 16t syba, 16–17 Andrei Merkulov, 16l Stefen Redel, 17tr Dean Mitchell, 17br Norman Pogson, 18l Kurt De Bruyn, 18br Tyler Olson, 19tr Stephen Finn, 19l Leah-Anne Thompson, 19br David Roos, 20t Mikael Damkier, 20bl Tyler Olson, 21br David Hyde, 23br Enika Balogh, 26–27 Elena Elisseeva, 26r italianestro, 26l matka_Wariatka, 27r Destiny VisPro, 28t Stanislav Popov, 28l iofoto, 28r Rafa Irusta, 28b Bryan Buscoicki, 29br Terrance Emerson

The words in **bold** are explained in the glossary on page 30.

LEEDS LIBRARIES AND INFORMATION SERVICE	
LD 4113003 0	
HJ	23-Nov-2009
551.6	£12.99
S035177	

Contents

What is weather?

When you wake up in the morning, the first thing you notice is the weather! Hot, cold, sunshine or rain – weather can change every day.

Changing weather

There is a huge range of weather around the world. Some places have more calm periods than others, or more or less sunshine, cloud, rain, wind, snow or ice. They have more or fewer storms, **floods** and **droughts**. In some places, weather conditions change quickly. There might be freezing fog, then warm sunshine, then clouds and rain, all in one day!

Some places have extreme weather. A snowfall covers everything in sight.

Hurricanes can flood whole cities, causing serious damage to people's homes.

↑ Satellite pictures show the swirling air of hurricanes. from high above the Earth.

Woolly mammoths died out about 4000 years ago.

📷 **FOCUS ON**

Ice Ages

Climates have changed many times in the past. During ice ages the whole world was much colder. The last Ice Age started about 50,000 years ago and finished 10,000 years ago. In frozen northern lands, woolly mammoths and rhinos had thick fur coats to protect them from the cold.

Climates

Weather is what happens day by day. **Climate** is the average weather conditions over a much longer time — years and centuries. A **tropical** climate is hot all of the time. A **polar** climate is very cold most of the time.

↑ In a polar climate, there is snow and ice all year round.

↖ In a tropical, dry climate, there is hot sunshine for most of the day.

WORLDclimates

The Earth has different climate areas, or zones.
There are different zones around the North Pole,
South Pole and near the Equator.

KEY
- Permanent ice
- Polar
- Cool temperate
- Desert
- Warm temperate
- Tropical
- Mountains

ARCTIC CIRCLE

NORTH AMERICA

EUROPE

TROPIC OF CANCER

AFRICA

EQUATOR

SOUTH AMERICA

TROPIC OF CAPRICORN

ANTARCTIC CIRCLE

Wet and dry areas

Near the Equator, the climate is warm. Where it is wet, thick tropical **rainforests** grow. Further north and south, there are dry **deserts**. **Temperate** climates are found between the tropics and the poles. These have warm summers and cold, wet winters.

⟳ *The closer an area is to the Equator, the hotter the temperature is because the Sun's rays are more direct.*

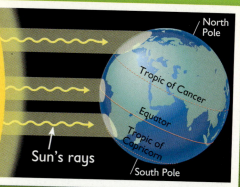

Rays are spread out away from the Equator ⇨

Rays are focused ⇨ at the Equator

Sun's rays

North Pole
Tropic of Cancer
Equator
Tropic of Capricorn
South Pole

Cold and hot regions

Tropical regions are warmest. The Sun is high above and its strong rays beat straight down. Polar regions are coldest. In the far north and south, the Sun is low in the sky, even at midday. Its rays are spread over a wide angle, so their heat is spread over a much greater area.

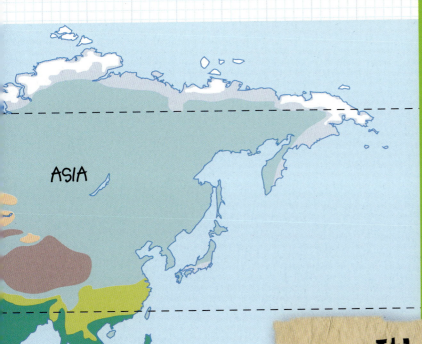

ASIA

OCEANIA

🜁 *The coloured areas show different world climate zones on land. The climate at sea may be windier and less rainy than on land.*

ANTARCTICA

It's a wonder!

In the hottest deserts, almost no life can survive.

The average temperature in the Arctic during winter is about -30 degrees Celsius.

Temperature measures hot and cold. Most people feel comfortable at 21–22 degrees Celsius. The hottest temperature ever recorded was in Libya, Africa – almost 58 degrees Celsius. The coldest was on Antarctica – -89 degrees Celsius.

Global greenhouse

A greenhouse has a clear glass roof and walls. Inside, it is usually warmer than outside, especially on a sunny day. This is because the glass traps heat from the Sun inside the greenhouse. The air that surrounds the Earth acts in the same way as the glass in a greenhouse.

Keeping in heat

The layer of air around the Earth is called the atmosphere. It lets most of the Sun's rays pass through it, to the Earth's surface. The atmosphere also traps some of the heat from these rays, stopping them from escaping into space. This trapped heat keeps the Earth warm. This is called the greenhouse effect.

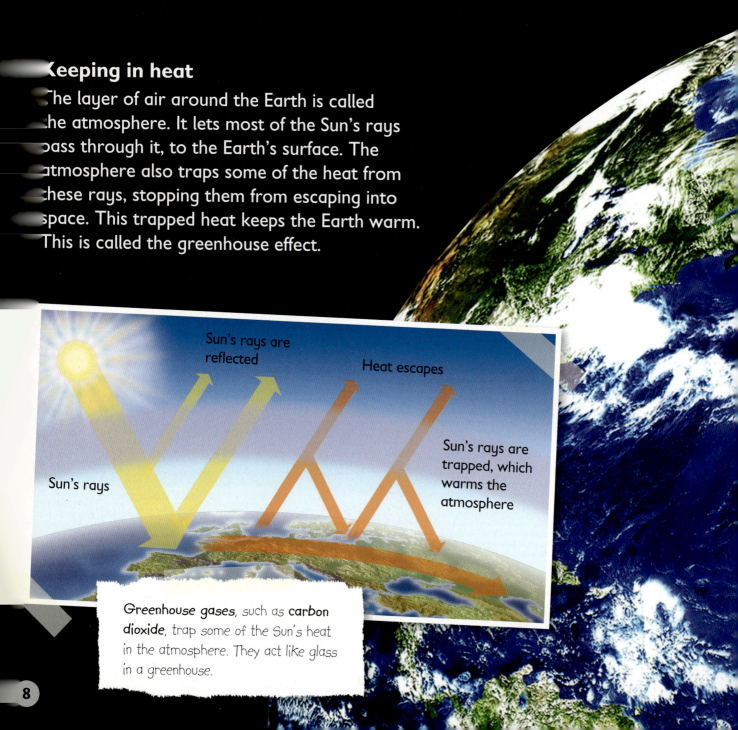

Sun's rays are reflected

Heat escapes

Sun's rays are trapped, which warms the atmosphere

Sun's rays

Greenhouse gases, such as carbon dioxide, trap some of the Sun's heat in the atmosphere. They act like glass in a greenhouse.

Natural balance

The Earth's natural greenhouse effect has been working for millions of years. With it, the average world temperature is 15 degrees Celsius. Without it, the temperature would be less than 0 degrees Celsius, with ice almost everywhere. The problem today is that we are altering the natural balance of the Earth's greenhouse effect.

The atmosphere stretches to about 100 kilometres above the Earth – that's more than 330 Eiffel Towers high!

It's a wonder!

Venus is far too hot for any form of life to survive there.

The Earth is not the only planet with a greenhouse effect. On Venus, temperatures can reach up to 480 degrees Celsius. This is so hot that a piece of wood would catch fire by itself!

A time of change

For centuries, scientists have measured temperatures and other weather conditions on Earth. These conditions are changing, which is having a great effect on nature.

Global warming

Temperatures are measured daily, at thousands of weather stations worldwide, from high in the mountains to far out at sea. The results show that, almost everywhere, the Earth's climate is slowly getting hotter. Average temperatures are rising and the world is warmer than it was 100 years ago. This is called **global warming**. If this continues, in 100 years, Earth will be a very different place.

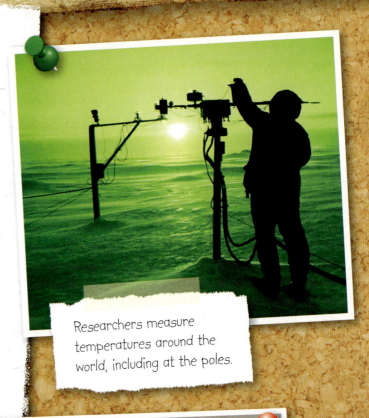

Researchers measure temperatures around the world, including at the poles.

➲ *Weather stations vary in size, from a small box to a big building. They measure many weather conditions, including temperature, rainfall, wind and sunshine.*

Nature knows

The natural world shows signs of global warming, too. Flowers come out earlier because winter becomes spring sooner. This also means that they die sooner and animals that normally feed on them are left with no food. Insects that were only found in the hot tropics are spreading around the world – and carrying dangerous **diseases** such as malaria with them. In cold places, ice sheets and glaciers are melting.

📷 FOCUS ON

Glaciers

Rivers of ice are called glaciers. They flow very slowly down high mountain slopes and in cold lands. They usually move about 1-2 metres a year. Due to global warming, glaciers are starting to melt. In the future, this could cause low-lying land to flood.

🎧 *Flowers such as daffodils are coming out earlier each year, when there is still snow on the ground.*

Where glaciers meet the sea, chunks of ice break off as icebergs. As this ice melts, sea levels rise.

Climate culprits

The reason that the Earth is getting warmer is that we are changing its 'glass' – the gases that surround it. The natural greenhouse effect is becoming unbalanced.

Greenhouse gases

Earth's atmosphere is made of a mixture of gases. One is **oxygen**, which we need to breathe to stay alive. Another is **water vapour**, one of the main natural greenhouse gases. It soaks up the Sun's heat and holds onto it. Water vapour can make the air feel moist and clammy.

Wht Cn U do ?

Turn off lights when they're not being used. This saves electricity, so power stations don't need to make as much.

↻ Smoke, fumes and vapours from power stations add to the greenhouse gases in the air.

Too much

One very important greenhouse gas is carbon dioxide. It forms only a tiny amount of the atmosphere. However, the amount is rising, mainly because when we burn fuels such as coal, petrol, gas and wood, we make carbon dioxide. Its global warming effects are powerful.

⬆ Water vapour in the air turns into tiny water droplets, which form clouds.

It's a wonder!

Scientists use weather balloons to measure temperature and the amount of water vapour in the air.

Many of the warmest years measured by scientists have been in the past 15 years. Almost everywhere in the world, the climate is changing.

Fossil fuels

Fossil fuels are coal, oil and natural gas, and fuels made from them, such as petrol and diesel. They contain a substance called carbon. When carbon burns, it forms the greenhouse gas carbon dioxide.

In the rocks

A fossil is the remains of something once alive, such as an animal or plant, preserved in the rocks. Fossils take millions of years to form. Many fossils have been found, including giant shark teeth and plants.

➲ Fossils have formed from all kinds of dead materials, such as dinosaur bones.

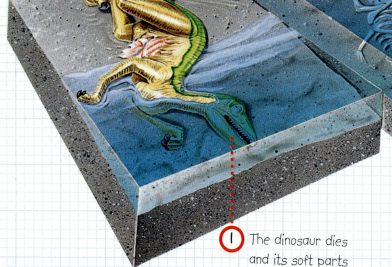

① The dinosaur dies and its soft parts rot away.

② Sand and mud bury the hard bone.

③ More layers collect on top as the bones turn to stone.

Coal, oil and gas

Lumps of coal are the hard, black fossil remains of giant plants that grew on Earth more than 300 million years ago. Thick, sticky oil in the ground is the remains of tiny sea creatures and plants that also lived millions of years ago. Natural gas deep underground was made in a similar way to oil, but it became a gas, not a liquid.

Oil rigs at sea hold giant drills that reach oil deep under the seabed.

5 Fossils are found at the surface.

4 Rocks are worn away by weather and earth movement.

It's a wonder!

Next time you see a lump of coal, ask an adult to split it open. You may see shapes of leaves – these are fossils from millions of years ago.

Coal can contain fossilized animals and plants, such as fern leaves.

Burning fuels

Every day, people around the world burn large amounts of fossil fuels. This produces huge quantities of carbon dioxide. It also uses up fossil fuels we cannot replace.

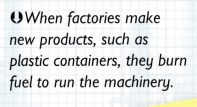
When factories make new products, such as plastic containers, they burn fuel to run the machinery.

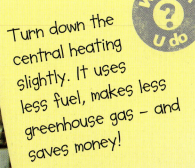

Turn down the central heating slightly. It uses less fuel, makes less greenhouse gas – and saves money!

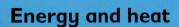

Energy and heat

Fuels contain lots of energy. Burning them releases this energy as heat. We use this heat in many ways – warming our homes, in the engines of cars and other vehicles, in aeroplane jet engines, in **power stations** to produce electricity and in factories to make products such as paper, glass and steel.

Two problems

Our modern way of life depends on burning fossil fuels. However, there are two problems. One problem is that they emit, or give off, carbon dioxide, which adds to global warming. The other problem is that fossil fuels are running out. We use them millions of times faster than they can form. If we keep using oil at the present rate, in 100 years there will be almost none left.

Vehicle engines use fossil fuels and pollute the air.

Greenhouse gases

Carbon emissions produced when we burn fossil fuels cause up to one quarter of the global warming effect. Other greenhouse gases include methane and ozone.

Smelly methane

Methane is part of natural gas. It's also made by cows when they digest food. It comes out of their mouths and their rear ends. As we raise more cattle, they put more methane into the atmosphere. Methane is also produced by rotting rubbish heaps and landfills. Methane causes up to one-seventh of global warming.

At landfill sites, huge pits are dug in the ground and the waste is buried.

You can usually find somewhere to recycle near your house.

Repair, reuse and recycle. This way, you save raw materials and energy, cause less **pollution** and reduce the rubbish in landfills.

Wht Cn U do?

Ozone

Ozone is a form of oxygen. When strong sunlight shines on exhaust fumes from cars, ozone forms and can make it hard for us to breathe. However, high in the sky ozone is useful. A layer of ozone protects the Earth from the harmful rays of the Sun. **Manmade chemicals** are destroying this ozone layer.

In some cities, there is a layer of **smog** sitting in the air.

Changing world

As global warming causes the climate to change, our world will alter in many ways. Scientists believe that there will be other problems besides warmer weather.

Farms and food

Changing climates will also affect our farms and food. Regions that grow vast fields of wheat, corn and other crops could become too wet or dry. As **grasslands** dry out, cattle and other farm animals could starve. In the sea, changes in water temperature mean there are fewer fish, so we cannot catch as many as we have been.

⋂ *Cutting down trees destroys natural habitats, and affects the climate because trees take in harmful carbon dioxide.*

In dry countries, people have to dig very deep wells to find water, and pump it to the surface. Water may become more scarce in the future.

📷 FOCUS ON

El Niño

Every few years, the waters and atmosphere of the Pacific Ocean undergo a change called El Niño. This produces many effects, from bigger storms to smaller fish catches. No one knows how climate change will affect El Niño.

When El Niño takes place, there are more storms and extreme weather.

Climate zones

Places that used to be rainy might get drier. Places that were once dry could be wetter. Some regions might get hotter, but a few could be cooler. As lakes dry out and deserts flood, wild animals and plants will face huge problems.

↻ Climate change could mean that farmland will become hard and dry.

WEATHER warning

As climates change, there may be more extreme weather, such as storms, floods, hurricanes, heatwaves and droughts.

Stormy weather

Over the last few years, there have been more hurricanes and other big storms around the world. As oceans get warmer, the storms become bigger, with stronger winds and more rain.

Hurricane Katrina filled the streets of New Orleans, USA, with water.

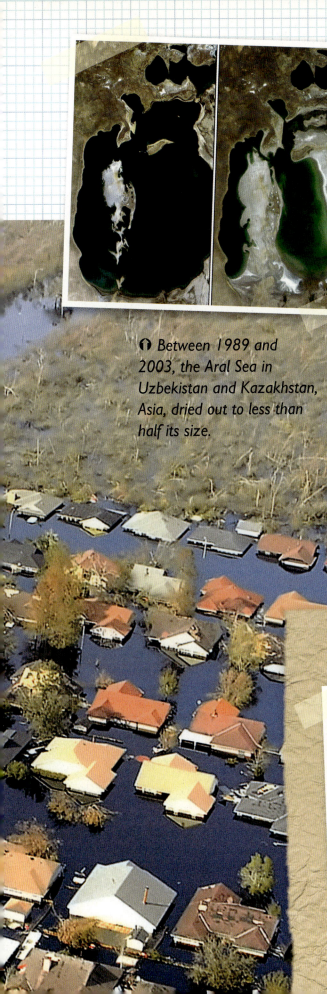

Heating up

On average, heatwaves and droughts are increasing. The Aral Sea in Central Asia and Lake Chad in Africa are just two watery places that are shrinking fast. People around them take water for their homes, factories and farms. If climate change continues to make land drier around the world, the need for water will increase.

🎧 *Between 1989 and 2003, the Aral Sea in Uzbekistan and Kazakhstan, Asia, dried out to less than half its size.*

Destruction

In 2005, Hurricane Katrina flooded the city of New Orleans, USA. In 2008, Cyclone Nargis flooded a massive area of Burma. More than 150,000 people died. High winds wreck buildings, and floods ruin farmland and cities.

It's a wonder!

Hurricane Katrina's fastest winds were 280 kilometres an hour, which is 2.5 times the motorway speed limit!

Rising sea levels

Global warming means that seas and oceans will get warmer. When things get warmer they expand, or get bigger. As the sea expands, the water level will rise.

Flood warning

Sea levels rise each year by one to 2 millimetres — almost the height of this 'o'. In the next 100 years they could rise more than one metre. That's enough to flood huge coastal ports and cities, and large amounts of low-lying farmland near the shore.

🎧 Since 1997, Tepukasavilivili Island in the Pacific Ocean has started to disappear because sea levels are rising.

Every minute, lumps of glaciers melt into the sea, making water levels rise.

Ice reflects many
of the Sun's rays
back into space

Sun

Light and heat
rays hit ice

Ice

Sea

As ice melts, less of the
Sun's heat goes back
into space, and global
warming speeds up.

Water takes in
heat and reflects
fewer rays

FOCUS ON 📷

Mirror effect

Shiny white snow
and ice reflect,
or bounce back,
the Sun's light and
heat. As they melt,
they reflect less
of the Sun's rays.
The heat stays in
the atmosphere, which
adds to global warming.

Melting ice

Melting ice also affects sea levels. There
are massive amounts of ice in the towering
glaciers and icebergs of Alaska, Greenland
and Siberia in the north, and even more
in Antarctica in the south. If it all melted
tomorrow, sea levels around the world
would rise by more than 50 metres.

Slow the change

There are many ways we can help to reduce global warming and slow climate change. If we all play a small part, it will add up to make a big difference.

Green solution

Carbon dioxide is good for plants. All plants need to take it in from the atmosphere. They combine it with energy from sunlight, to live and grow and make fruits and seeds. This process is called photosynthesis.

↻ *Plants take in excess carbon dioxide and give out oxygen, so they are very important to the environment.*

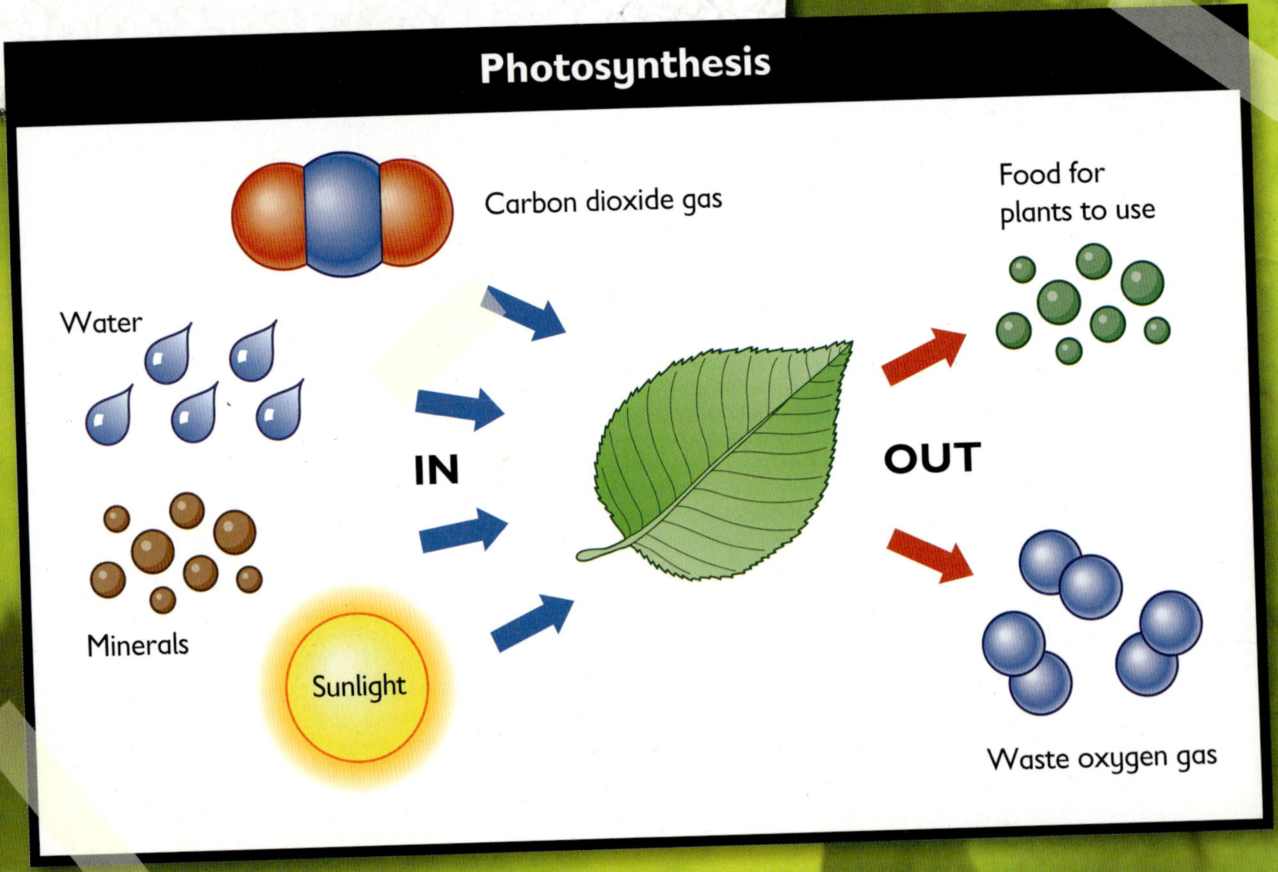

Photosynthesis

Carbon dioxide gas

Water

Minerals

Sunlight

IN

OUT

Food for plants to use

Waste oxygen gas

More means less

The more trees and other plants we have, the more carbon dioxide they use up, so the less there is for global warming. As we cut down trees, the opposite happens. This is why it's important to save woodlands, forests and other natural places, and to plant more trees.

⮫ *The carbon cycle shows how carbon is constantly used and reproduced. By cutting down trees, the cycle becomes unbalanced.*

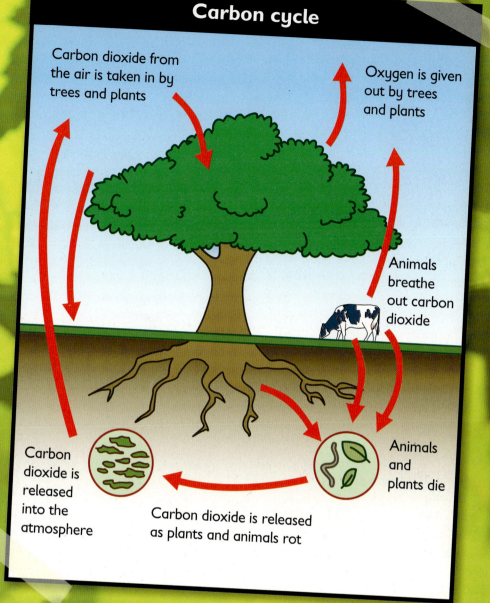

Carbon cycle

Carbon dioxide from the air is taken in by trees and plants

Oxygen is given out by trees and plants

Animals breathe out carbon dioxide

Carbon dioxide is released into the atmosphere

Carbon dioxide is released as plants and animals rot

Animals and plants die

Cycle, walk or take the bus or train, rather than a car.

Wht Cn ? U do

Keep it cool

Most scientists agree that global warming and climate change have begun, and we must act fast to make it slow down.

⟳ Wind is a free, long-term source of energy for electricity.

Hydroelectricity produces no greenhouse gases or pollution.

Alternative electricity

Two-thirds of the world's electricity comes from burning fossil fuels. We can support **alternative energy**, such as hydroelectric dams and wind turbines. **Nuclear power** stations produce little carbon dioxide, but they create other problems such as dangerous **radioactive** waste.

⟲ The Hoover Dam on the border of Arizona and Nevada, USA, works by using huge generators. The generators are powered using the water.

A farmers' market sells local fresh produce. The food does not travel far.

Wht Cn ? U do

- Buying food grown locally is one way to reduce our carbon footprint and travel miles.
- 'Carbon footprint' shows the carbon emissions a particular lifestyle produces.
- 'Travel miles' show how far goods and products travel, which produces carbon emissions.

Be aware

We must learn about global warming and try to change the way we live before it is too late. Governments and industries are trying to find ways to produce everything we need without harming the planet.

 **FOCUS ON**

Biofuels

Crops can be used to make fuel for vehicles – called biofuel. The plants take in carbon dioxide as they grow and burning the fuel produces it. Some people do not support biofuel production because either trees are cut down to grow the crop or the farmland could be used to grow food crops.

Corn is often harvested to create biofuel.

Glossary

Alternative energy Energy that is produced in ways that do not damage or pollute the environment. Alternative energy cannot run out.

Carbon dioxide A gas that is naturally present in tiny amounts in air. It is produced by burning, and acts as a powerful greenhouse gas.

Carbon emissions The emission, or giving off, of gases that contain carbon, especially carbon dioxide.

Climate The average pattern of temperature, rainfall, winds and other weather conditions in a particular place over hundreds or thousands of years.

Desert A very dry place that has little or no rain.

Disease An illness or sickness that causes problems in the body, makes people feel unwell and may cause death.

Drought A unusually long period of time without rain.

Equator An imaginary band around the middle of the Earth, halfway between the North Pole and the South Pole.

Flood Too much water in a place that usually has little or no water.

Fossil Any part of a dead plant or animal that has been preserved in rock.

Global warming The rise in the temperature of the atmosphere. It is caused by increased amounts of greenhouse gases, which are produced when burning fuels.

Grassland A habitat, such as the North American prairies or African savanna, where the main plants are grasses.

Greenhouse gas A gas that traps the Sun's heat and makes the atmosphere around the Earth warmer.

Heatwave An unusually long period of high temperatures.

Hurricane A large powerful storm with fast winds that swirl round and lots of heavy rain.

Hydroelectricity Electricity that is made using moving water.

Manmade chemicals Substances made by humans that may have harmful effects. For example, chemical sprays for farm crops that kill weeds or pests.

Methane A gas made when things rot or when animals digest food.

Nuclear power Electricity that is made by splitting or breaking apart the centres of atoms.

Oxygen A gas that makes up one-fifth of the air around us. Humans and animals breathe oxygen to stay alive.

Polar The region around the North Pole or the South Pole, at the top or bottom of the Earth, where it is cold all year round.

Pollution When harmful substances such as chemicals or litter get into the surroundings and cause damage.

Power station A building that has machines called generators to make electricity.

Radioactive Giving off harmful rays, called radiation, that can cause serious illness, burns and even death.

Rainforest A forest where it rains on most days throughout the year.

Smog Polluted air that looks like a mixture of smoke and fog. It is caused by burning fuels in cars and factories.

Temperate Not too hot or too cold.

Tropical The region around the middle of the Earth, on either side of the Equator, where it is warm all year.

Water vapour Water in the form of a gas, which is invisible and floats in the air.

Weather Conditions such as the temperature, amount of rain and wind strength, and how these conditions change from day to day and week to week.

Index